MW01291514

HOW TO GROW

LAVENDER

FLOWER & CARE

A STEP BY STEP GUIDE

GEORGE BEST

COPY RIGHT© 2019

GEORGE BEST

This book may not be reproduced, distributed or transmitted by any means without the prior written consent of the author first had and obtained. The facts herein provided is truthful in all its entirety and coherent, in that no legal responsibility, in the form of consideration or else by the use or misuse of any strategies, procedures or directions contained within shall lie against the author such liability thereon is the sole and the utter obligation of the reader solely. Under no situation will any legal duty or blames be imputed or held out unfavorable the publisher(s) for any form of compensation, damages, pecuniary loss due to the information contained herein be it direct or indirect.

TABLE OF CONTENTS

CHAPETR ONE

PRELUDE TO LAVENDER FLOWERS

Lavenders are flowering plants of the mint family that are easily identify by their sweet floral scents. They are spike-like flowers made up of multiple, small purple flowers or "florets" on long narrow stems. Lavender flowers are believed to be indigenous to the native of the Mediterranean, Middle East and Indian. It has an ancient history dating back to as far as over 2500 years ago. Lavender has been known for its gentle and soothing fragrance since ancient times. It had been used by Greeks and Romans in the public baths. The name 'lavender' is derived from the Latin word "lavare", which means "to wash". The Latin name for lavender is "Lavendula angustifolia"

Lavender has been used as a holy herb since ancient times and it have also been valued for centuries and was often used to give a light scent to a variety of personal items, for their physical beauty, healing properties, soothing fragrance, and several other uses of lavender flowers. In addition to these characteristics, lavender flowers also possess a unique meaning.

As a strewing herb, it does not only offers a pleasing scent to us, but also helps to repels insects. Lavender was also used to mask the scent of unpleasant smells in the streets of old and it still a universally delicate and lovely scent for households worldwide.

Just like other flowers, Lavender flowers also have common meanings associated to them. The list of some of the most common meanings for Lavender flowers; Grace, Silence, Calmness, Purity, Devotion, Serenity and Caution

As a flowers, Lavender has a purple colour and the colour purple from time past has been associated with the crown chakra, which is any of the several points of physical or spiritual energy in the human body {this is according to yoga philosophy}. The crown which is also known as the 7th chakra is located at the top of the head and the highest vibration in the physical body is the vibration of the crown. This expression is appropriate as the Lavender flowers are often used for healing purposes and elevating our vibration to the highest level possible is one of the easiest path to healing.

Lavender before now, has been used extensively in aromatherapy and for treatment of minor injuries. Lavender infusions are accepted to bring calmness to burns, insect bites, acne, headaches and inflammatory conditions. Bunches of lavender flowers are also known to be insects repellent. Research has also shown that Lavender seeds and flowers aid sleep and relaxation. Also, an infusion of lavender flower-heads to a cup of boiling water is used to soothe and relax at bedtime.

Lavender essential oil is approved for use as an anxiolytic {a drug that relieves anxiety} in Germany under the name Lasea. According to a survey paper on lavender and the nervous system which was published in the year 2013, has this to say; "there is growing evidence suggesting that lavender oil may be an effective medicament in treatment of several neurological disorders." Although researches in this regards are limited.

Lavender flowers grows very well in sunny, open areas. They loves well-drained soil, slightly sweet. This also can be created in a less ideal soils, with the addition of lime. Lavender plants are very hard to propagate from seed, and it is best to buy established plants from a hotbed.

THE NEED FOR LAVENDER IN YOUR HOME

Lavender in our world today is more than just a fragrant plant. As researches has shown, lavender are also used for medicinal and therapeutic benefits. They are herbs that are native to northern Africa and the mountainous regions of the Mediterranean. They are also believed to have antiseptic and anti-inflammatory properties that can help in the treatment of minor burns and bugs bites. This section of this book shall focus on the various benefits that one can get through having lavender flowers or the consist use of lavender essential oil. It is important that you pay close attention to all the health benefits that will be explained and the possible way of achieving some of them.

AIR PURIFICATION

Because of the special features that lavender plants possess and the aromatic fragrance that emanates from it, your home will be free from chemical substances created from your electronic devices, cooking items, air conditioner, and other chemicals that are carried through your windows into your home.

Apart from the sweet fragrance ability of lavender plants you enjoy in your home, they also improve the quality of air. Lavender plant improves air quality as during photosynthesis, they absorb carbon dioxide and convert it into oxygen which is essential for the human body. A study carried by scientist established that plants like lavender remove chemical pollutants in the air and increase the level of oxygen which gives you a very healthy home or office environment.

Exotic Look

Lavender are generally exotic in their look. They come in different amazing sizes and shapes. The different species of lavender have their different looks, although they all looks similar and beautiful. Their exotic look however, is seen more when you place them in a container or in a pot within your garden.

Environmental Beautification

The more peaceful, relax, and beautiful your environment where you spend your resting time in the mornings, evenings and weekends is, the more your ability to manage the stress that you have gathered during the course of the week activities. A visible advantage of having lavender flower in your home is that it can beautify your environment and the visible appearance of your home. You can join your lavender with some objects in your home to give them a perfect outlook. Lavender plants creates a very warm environment for your home. The greatest aspect of this plant is when they are expertly kept in flowering pot and specially placed at the entrance of the house for captivating appearance.

Lavender Improve Better Sleep

Lavender inhalation can help with insomnia {the condition of not being able to sleep} and improve sleep quality by reducing stress response and lowering resting heart rate. Insomnia is a nagging problem that keeps you awake, tossing and turning throughout the night. Lavender oil increases you sleep efficiency by allowing deeper and longer. When you reduce your caffeine consumption and add more exercise, it might also help to induce sleep. At times, these efforts and others remedies does not work. Given to lack of proper sleep at night, you end up a groggy mess during the daytime.

If insomnia is your problem and you are willing to try something new for a restful night's sleep, a research work published in March 2017 in the British Association of Critical Nurses found out that "lavender essential oil is an effective remedy in improving the sleep quality of intensive care unit (ICU) patients who had difficulty sleeping". Also, the brain of ten healthy women who were exposed to lavender odour was examined by scientist and it was discovered that lavender increases both brain arousal and feelings of relaxations.

Maybe you have tried other sleep remedies and all to no avail, why not try lavender essential oil. It is very simple, get lavender essential oil and place a few drops on your pillow before going to sleep tonight. Take care not to ingest it, or any other essential oil, this is because by so doing, you may pose health harms.

Lavender Help Treat Skin Blemishes

Just like other variety of essential oils, lavender is also excellent for dermatology use. For those suffering from skin inflammation, acne, or eczema, applying lavender essential oil to the affected spot could play a major role in treating blemishes and ease inflammation. This is according to a study that was published in May 2017 in the journal Evidence-Based Complementary and Alternative Medicine. If your skin is very sensitive, it is important that you dilute the essential oil in a carrier oil or water.

Also, the antioxidant activity of lavender could contribute to the healing of wounds.

It is also important that you consult your dermatologist before adding lavender essential oil to your skincare regimen, this is to make sure that it doesn't interact with any of the medication that you are currently taking.

Lavender Reduce Stress

Too much stress on the heart that is, as result of chronic high blood pressure puts the health of our heart at risk of several complications such as stroke and heart attack. These health concerns can however be moderated and controlled. Lavender oil decreases heart rate, blood pressure and body temperature, indicating a decrease in the flight or fight response. A research paper, published in 2017 in the Iranian Journal of Pharmaceutical Research discovered that "when 40 people inhaled lavender essential oil after open-heart surgery, they reduced their blood pressure and heart rate, suggesting the oil had a positive effect on their vital signs". This was however not conclusive as the authors noted that more research is required on this possible benefit namely, "a randomized controlled trial, the gold standard for medical research, with a larger sample size".

Lavender Help Relieve Asthma Symptoms

Given to the anti-inflammatory properties of lavender, they may also help to improve bronchial asthma. A research work on mice, which was published in July 2014 in the journal Life Sciences discovered that "lavender essential oil had a positive impact on respiratory health, relieving allergic inflammation and mucus hyperplasia".

Although this research is inclusive because whether the same effect would be obtainable in humans remains unclear.

Lavender Lessens Menopausal Hot Flashes

A common menopause symptom that affects several women are hot flashes or hot flushes. This often causes a sudden feeling of heat over their body, which can make the face flushed and also trigger perspiration.

But when you use lavender aromatherapy for about twenty {20} minutes and twice a day, it could help to reduce menopause flashing and improve quality of life. This is according to a research work published in the Journal of Chinese Medical Association in September 2016.

Lavender Help Combat Fungus Growth

There are reasonable numbers of researches highlighting the potential antifungal properties of lavender. A study that was published in the Journal of Medical Microbiology discovered that lavender essential could be effective in combating antifungal resistant infections. Other researchers suggest that lavender essential oil could be effective in inhibiting the growth of certain types of fungus, such as C. albicans. Lavender essential oil can also act as a remedy for the treatment of ringworm and athlete's foot, which are also caused by fungus, according to another research.

Lavender Help Promotes Hair Growth

Lavender is possibly an effective means of treating alopecia areata {this is a situation of hair loss in some or all areas of ones body}. Studies have shown that lavender can promote the growth of hair by 44 percent between seven months of treatment. In yet another research, application of lavender essential oil to the backs of mice once a day, 5 times a week, for 4 weeks, saw an increase in their number of hair follicles and a thicker dermal layer. With this, researchers were made to believe that lavender oil could potentially be used as agent for promoting hair growth, although more researches are still needed in this regards since mouse are not human beings.

CHAPTER TWO

LAVENDER SPECIES FOR YOU

ENGLISH LAVENDER

Lavandula Angustifolia

The English lavender is also known as True lavender, and her scientific name is known as Lavandula angustifolia. It is the most widely grown type of lavender in North America, this is because this specie of lavender doesn't mind humidity and winter moisture as much as some other lavenders does. This lavender is an evergreen and slow-growing perennial plant, which usually attain the height of 3 feet and has a short and slightly crooked stem.

English lavender usually have narrow leaves and are between grey-green to blue-green in colour, while its flowers are barrel-shaped and this lavender comes in an array of different colours, it has purple and pink, to pale purple, lilac, and even white. English lavender is a hardy plant and it is a drought resistant. The sweet fragrance and floral scent of this lavender flowers make them ideal for making sachets and perfumes.

'Hidcote' English Lavender

This is one of the most popular English lavenders that you can find around, 'Hidcote' lavenders supplies silvery leaves with dark purple-blue flowers from late spring to early summer. They are good choice for small gardens. 'Hidcote' is also one of the strongest-scented varieties of English lavender. Her botanical name is Lavandula angustifolia 'Hidcote'. They are usually 24 inches tall and 30 inches wide

'Purple Bouquet' English Lavender

The 'Purple Bouquet' lavender have silvery-green foliage, long stems, and flower heads which are packed with rich purple blooms in early summer, this variety of lavender is a good choice if your desire is to grow lavender for cutting fresh or drying.

As common with other types of lavender, this variety of lavender grows better on the dry side. In growing this lavender, try to raise in beds or on mounds to increase drainage. Her botanical name is Lavandula angustifolia 'Purple Bouquet', and they are 20 inches tall and 30 inches wide

'Graves' English Lavender

This type of English lavender offers gardeners wonderfully, lovely fragrant

lavender-blue flowers in the late spring and early summer. This type of lavender is a heavy bloomer and grows a little taller than many of the other types of English lavenders that haven been known.

If you like or order this variety of lavender and you have a clay soil, ensure that you amend soil with an abundance of compost or any other form of organic matter before you plant your 'Graves' lavender or even so for other types of lavenders. Her botanical name is Lavandula angustifolia 'Graves' and they are 36 inches tall and 30 inches wide

'Munstead' English Lavender

Several gardeners have referred to 'Munstead lavender' as their favourite type of lavender, this is because this type of lavender is quite compact and it displays violet-purple flowers between mid to late spring, and it shows off an attractive silvery leaves. Just like the 'Hidcote', 'Munstead is known for her strong fragrance. They are 18 inches tall and 24 inches wide and her botanical is Lavandula angustifolia 'Munstead'

'Betty's Blue' English Lavender

The Betty's blue lavender outstanding because of its adaptable habit: This type of lavender is grows in a decidedly rounded mound and they produces large spikes of dark purple-blue flowers between the late spring and early summer. This type of lavender is a compact variety and they shines when they are grown as a small hedge or in a knot garden. They are 30 inches tall and 36 inches wide and her botanical name is Lavandula angustifolia 'Betty's Blue'

'Buena Vista' English Lavender

This type of lavender is a choice variety that blooms twice a year. The first is in late spring, while the other in autumn with a few flower spikes appearing in between. The Buena Vista has a bicolored purple and violet flowers features.

When growing 'Buena Vista' lavenders in containers as well as other lavender, make sure that the containers have several drainage holes to allow excess water to escape. Her botanical name is Lavandula angustifolia 'Buena Vista' and they are 28 inches tall and 36 inches wide

'Croxton's Wild' English Lavender

This type of lavender is similar to the wild lavender that is found in the Mediterranean. This lavender specie shows off light violet and purple flowers between late spring and early summer and has a loose, open form. They are 24 inches tall and 36 inches wide and her botanical name is Lavandula angustifolia 'Croxton's Wild'

'Royal Purple' English Lavender

Choose the 'Royal Purple' lavender for her long early-summer stems of strongly scented purple flowers. This type of lavender's blooms hold their colour well after drying. 'Royal Purple' is one of the larger English lavenders plant you can grow as a stunning low, informal hedge.

When you grow this type of lavender, leave space between plants so air flows freely. This variety of lavender plants as well other varieties are more susceptible to disease if they are too close to each other.

'Melissa' English Lavender

The 'Melissa' has something different: it provides light pink flowers that fade to white. Just like other type of English lavenders, 'Melissa' has silvery leaves and it blooms between late spring and early summer. The ideal time to prune this type of lavender as well as the other lavenders is back in the spring. They are usually 20 inches tall and 24 inches wide and her botanical name is Lavandula angustifolia 'Melissa'

'Lady'   English   Lavender

This is an All-America Selections award winner lavender that blooms the first year from seed, this is to say that you can grow Lady Lavender as an annual. This particular specie is compact and offers silvery-green leaf punctuated by spikes of purple-blue flowers during the summer.

'Jean Davis' English Lavender

The 'Jean Davis' lavender is a long-blooming lavender that produces pale pink flowers between the late spring and early to midsummer. 'Jean Davis' is a short variety that grows well in containers or the middle of the garden border. This variety is also known as Lavandula angustifolia 'Rosea'. This variety are usually 18 inches tall and 30 inches wide

FRENCH LAVENDER

The French lavender are commonly seen in the field of the province region in the south of France. They are grown more as an ornamental plant than as a beautiful garden flower. The French lavender does not emit the traditional fragrance (French lavender scent is more like camphor) like the English lavenders. But this is a lovely variety with clusters of purple flowers and furry, grey-green toothed foliage. The French lavender blooms all summer and fall, and can bloom almost throughout the year indoors if you have a bright window getting at least 6 hours of sun daily.

There are three varieties of French lavender and they are 'Provence', 'Grosso' and 'Fred Boutin'.

'Grosso' Lavandin

'Grosso' is a commonly grown variety of lavender in France. They provides a strongly scented rich purple flowers in midsummer among the most widely grown lavandins, and they also bloom a second time in autumn. They are cultivated for oil and are mainly used in the cosmetic industries. 'Grosso' Lavandin is a large variety that likes a lot of space but it makes a big impact. This is probably the most planted and cultivated variety of lavender across the world. 'Grosso' Lavandin plant gives the longest stems than any other variety grown and gives spectacular 2 feet+ dried stems with mid purple flowers. This can be less hardy in some areas.

Zones: 6-8

'Gros Bleu' Lavandin

The 'Gros Bleu' lavender is a common selection with long flower spikes and silvery leaves. They are loved for their rich purple flowers, and presents some of the darkest blooms than any other type of lavandin lavenders and they flowers profusely in summer. They are mostly 30 inches tall and 36 inches wide

Zones: 6-8

Provence Lavandin

If you reside in a humid area, the 'Provence' Lavandin is the best lavender plant for you to buy because they do great in those conditions. This is a lovely variety of lavender that offers light blue flowers on a narrow spikes in the summer. This variety is mostly grown commercially for its oil. It is one of the most fragrant lavender in the garden. In as much as it has a strong scent, its thin stems make 'Provence' a poor cut flower {although Provence are excellent for making lavender wands}

Zones: 6-8

SPANISH LAVENDER

When we talk about lavender, the first type of lavender that comes to people's mind is probably the English and French lavender. There are however other variety of lavender that exist and one of them is the Spanish lavender. The Spanish lavender plants, just like the English variety can give you the same aroma and delicate flowers. This variety are better able to tolerate hot climatic condition than the others. The Spanish lavender are native to the Mediterranean region and North Africa, this variety seems to be a more suitable lavender choice for those with garden in hot humid climates. Cultivating Spanish lavender is a good and better alternative to the more popular English lavender if you stay in a warmer climate.

Looking at them, the Spanish lavender is similar to the other varieties of lavender, growing in small shrubs that make great low hedges or bed borders. Spanish lavender have the same silvery-green leaves, but with a unique characteristic in how they flowers. The top of their flowering stem grows larger, upright bracts that looks like the rabbit ears. Her flowers may be pink or purple, it all depends on the cultivar. This variety lavender blooms profusely in the spring and when they finish blooming, they needs a good pruning. The result of the pruning will be an attractive, gray-green fragrant, shrub all through the remaining part of the year.

This variety of lavender is probably what the ancient Romans and Greeks used to scent their bath water. This is why the word 'Lavender' is from the Latin word 'lavare' which means 'to wash'. In older publications, Spanish Lavender is often referred to as French Lavender, which is today referred to Lavender dentata.

Spike Lavender Lavandula latifolia

As earlier mentioned, the most popular form of lavender herb is the English and French lavender. The Spike lavender with the botanical name of Lavandula latifolia, is also known as Portuguese lavender and they has spiked flowers and broad leaves. Spike lavender looks very similar to English lavender. The only difference is that their leaves are broader than the English lavender, and they has branched flower stalks. Latifola is the Latin name for "broadleaf." They can give about 3 times more essential oil than the English lavender, although this oil is not valued as valued as that of the English lavender.

This variety of lavender is native to the western Mediterranean, and can attain the height of 31 inches (80cm) tall. Whereas English lavender grows at a high altitudes, spike lavender prefers lower altitudes. The environmental differences is what is responsible for spike lavender to have a high concentration of camphor, which the English lavender lacks.

Cultivation of Spike lavender plant did not start until around 1925, although this was not as popular as other lavender species. Around 1950, the distillation of Spike lavender plant dwindled and artists went back to using the more economical turpentine.

Lavandin

Lavandin lavender is a hybrid of the English and the Spike lavender. This is also known as the Dutch lavender. This variety is a hardy, but slow-growing evergreen plant. They produces vibrant flowers from the beginning of midsummer, and this are mainly used for decorative purposes, and also for herbal crafts and potpourris. When they blossom, it can produce white, pink, or pale purple colour.

Lavandin flowers, as well as their foliage are highly fragrant. This variety of lavender plant yields more essential oil when compared to the English or other varieties of lavender, and her essential oil possesses a strong fragrance. Lavandin oil is used in a number of products, including perfumes, massage oils, toiletries, and several other household products.

CHAPTER THREE

LAVENDER FROM SEED

As noted in previous chapter, Lavender is a fragrant and beautiful herb that produces white, purple, and/or yellow flowers, depending on the variety that you have. Many of the numerous lavender gardeners often propagate lavender from cuttings, but lavender plant can also be grown from seed. Cultivating lavender flower from seed is not always successful and it is a fairly slow process, but using this method is often not too expensive when compared to buying cuttings or pre-started lavender plants and also, can eventually produce plants that are just as vibrant. If you are thinking of harvesting your own lavender seeds, you should know that some lavender plants won't produce seeds that are true to the plant.

STEP BY STEP GUIDE

Step 1

This first step in growing lavender from seed is to start the seeds 6 to 12 weeks before warm weather hits. The lavender seeds can take some time to germinate and it should be started early indoors, this is to give them plenty of time to grow into mature plants during the warm growing season. This is very important.

Step 2

The next line of action is to put your harvested seeds through a process called "cold stratifying." Put your harvested see s in between 2 wet paper towels, then add them to a sealable plastic bag. Keep the bag with the seeds in the refrigerator and allow it there for at least 21 days.

If you buy your seeds, you don't need to go through this process because it has already undergone through the process. You should only do this if your seeds are harvested by you from another plant.

Step 3

The following step is to fill your container with seed starting mix. Your seed starting mix should be a light potting mix that is well drained. You may choose to use a plastic seedling tray or a wide, shallow container that does not have divisions.

Step 4

When your seed starting mix is ready, sprinkle your seeds on top of the soil. You don't need to bury your seeds under the ground, but should however sprinkle a light layer of soil over the seeds.

When you are making use of a plastic seedling tray, plant one seed per slot. But if you are planting in a division-free container, space your seeds ½ to 1 inch apart.

Step 5

Cover your seeds with 1/8 inch potting mix. Use a light coating of potting mix to protect your seeds, but also make sure that the seeds have access to sunlight in order to germinate.

Step 6

Keep your seeds in a warm place. Use a heat tray this often works better, but for another location may work for as long as the temperature remains around 70 degrees Fahrenheit.

Step 7

Water your seeds lightly. Ensure that your growing medium is moist, but not damp, and do this in the morning so that your soil can dry off a bit before the evening hits. When your soil is too damp, it will invite fungus to grow, and fungus will destroy the seeds.

Step 8

Exercise patience for your seeds to sprout. When growing lavender from seeds, it can take between two weeks to one month for it to sprout. Watch your seeds while you wait for them to sprout. Ensure that your soil stays wet while you patiently wait for your seeds to sprout, and keep them in a sunny area.

Step 9

Expose your sprouted seeds plenty of light. Once your seeds has sprouted, it is important that you their containers to a location where they will receives plenty of direct sunlight. When you don't have such location, place a fluorescent grow light about your sprouts and allow them to sit in the artificial light for about eight hours daily.

TRANSPLANTING LAVENDER FLOWER

Step 1

To make your first lavender transplant, wait until your lavender plant gets it first sets of leaves. Exercise patience until the leaves are fully matured. At this point, the root of your lavender plant will have grown too large to continue sitting in a shallow tray.

Step 2

Get a larger container and fill it with a well-drained potting mix. There is no need for you to have seed starting mix, but should make your potting mix very light. Check out for mixes that are partly made of soil and partly peat, partly perlite. Peat moss are non-renewable resource, it is therefore better to use coir dust if possible. Be careful not use vermiculite, that may contain asbestos, even when it is not written on the label.

The pot you are using for each plant should at least be 2 inches in diameter (5 cm). Also, you can choose to use a division-free tray or a larger pot and space multiple lavender plants in the tray 2 inches apart from each other.

Step 3

Add little fertilizer to your soil. You can use a small amount of granular slow-release fertilizer which contains a balanced proportions of nitrogen, potassium, and phosphorus.

Step 4

Add the lavender to your prepared pot. Make a small hole in your fresh growing media which is about as big as the compartment your lavender is presently sitting in. Gently and carefully pry your lavender out of her original container and transplant them into the new hole, packing the soil around them to keep them firm and fixed to one place.

Step 5

Leave the lavender to keep on growing. Your lavender plants must attain a height of 3 inches (7.6 cm) before it can be transplanted to her final location, but it should still have only a single stem. This can happen as from one to three months of planting.

Step 6

Slowly introduce your lavender to outdoor conditions. Take your pots outdoors in a partial sun or partial shade for a few hours at a time, increasing their time outdoors little by little each day. Continue doing this for about one week, this will be long enough time for your lavender plant to adapt to outdoor conditions.

This process is referred to as "hardening off."

Step 7

Keep it in a sunny location. Lavender plants performs better when they are grown in full sun. Shaded areas tend to be soggier, and when the soil is soggy, it can invite fungi which will end up destroying your plant.

Step 8

Make ready your garden soil. Dip up the soil with a trowel or a digging fork to loosen the soil and mix in a healthy dose of compost. Compost particles are equal, therefore creating looser soil will make it easier for the roots of your lavender plant to stretch out. Also, when the soil is loosen, it allows water to flow freely.

It is important that you check your soil pH after adding compost. This should rest between 6 and 8, and it is better when it is between 6.5 and 7.5 for best results. When the soil pH is too low, mix in agricultural lime. When it is too high, add a small amount of plant litter pine sawdust.

If you stay in an area that has a damp winter or spring, there will be the need to plant your lavender on a mound. Once you dig out your hole, at the bottom mix gravel into the soil beneath the root ball. If the roots of your lavender plant is wet during the winter, your lavender plant will not survive.

Step 9

Transplant your lavender plants 12 - 24 inches apart (30 1/2 to 61 cm). Make a hole as deep as the container that your plant currently growing in. Take your lavender plant from the pot using a garden trowel to carefully slide it out, while you plant your lavender plant into the new hole.

CHAPTER FOUR

HOW TO GROW GARDEN LAVENDER

Since lavender plants are slow to germinate from seeds, buying seedling plants is the best way to grow this plant. Cultivating lavender plants is very easy if only you provide them with what they require to grow. It is true that lavender can tolerate a variety of growing conditions, as a plant, thrives best under warm and sunny conditions in a soil that is well-drained. In addition to a well-drained, a soil that is rich in alkaline organic matter will encourage higher plant oil production, and also increases the fragrance in lavender plants. Since lavender plant is native to arid regions, it will however not tolerate moist or overly wet conditions; it is therefore important that you consider your location when growing lavender plants. This plant should be located in areas with adequate drainage and far enough spaced to ensure good air circulation. When this is done, it will help to reduce the chances of developing root rot.

Make a hole and the soil removed from it, add a dusting of bonemeal to the hole, mixed in. Full the hole with water and leave it to drain away. Add your plant to the hole and fill to the level of the compost around the plant and firm in. when the condition dry, water the soil around the plant, and make sure that you do not over water it. It is much easier to water than you trying to dry out the soil. Pay close attention to plant in the first few weeks of planting, most especially when is a dry weather.

When growing lavender indoor, it should receive as much light as possible. Lavender do better in a south-facing window or where they can get at least three to four hours of direct sunlight each day. It is better for you to rotate the pot weekly for uniform growth and flowering. When there is no enough light, your lavender plant will produce a weak, spindly growth, it will cease to produce flowers, while they will be more susceptible to pest and disease.

It is important to have a good ventilation and air circulation, but be careful not place the plant where they will be exposed to the direct flow of forced-air heat. Ideal indoor temperatures from spring through mid-fall are 50 to 55 degrees F at night and 70 degrees F during the day. During the late fall through winter, temperatures should be cooler: 45 to 50 degrees F at night and 60 to 65 degrees F during the day.

When watering, it is important that you drench thoroughly and allow the soil to become slightly dry in between watering. Check your soil moisture by feeling the soil with fingers. When you over water your lavender and you allow your soil to stay moist constantly, it may result to rot of your plant. It is also important not to allow your soil to go completely dry, or if it does your lavender will react with yellowing lower leaves. When you moved your lavender outside in the spring, keep in mind that they will dry out more quickly and there will be the need to water then more frequently.

CARING FOR LAVENDER FLOWER

When thinking of growing lavender in your garden, you have to first of all try to discover the type of lavender that is suitable for growing in the climatic conditions of your region. The next essential step to take is to select a planting location that receives sunlight for about 7 to 8 hours each day. As noted earlier, lavender plants can both be grown from the seeds, as well as from the seedlings and they do better in a well-drained and slightly alkaline soil.

Just as it has been noted in our explanations, lavender plants needs little watering, especially when they have been established firmly to the ground. While they are young, they should be watered at regular intervals. When they are matured, lavender should also be watered regularly when the weather is extremely in dry conditions. To promote heat retention, you can apply a layer of sand around the base of the plant. This layer of sand will help to promote the production of better blooms in your lavender.

Lavender just like other flowers, grows great in large containers, and because they can grow quite large, it is good that you start with a large pot, at least 12 - 16 inches wide, this is to help you in accommodating the fierce growth.

When growing them in pot, it is good that you fill the bottom an 2 inches with packing peanuts. Apart from this expediting drainage, it will also help to keep the pot from getting too heavy to carry.

Mix your potting soil with a tablespoon of lime. Add enough soil in order for your potted lavender to sit about one inch about the soil line.

Also add additional soil and some fertilizer pellets to your remaining topsoil.

Layer this with white landscaping pebbles, that will reflects light and aids plant growth, and also, you keep the area around the base of your plant dry.

Keep your potted lavender plants in an area with full-sun for it to receive at least 8 hours of sun per day.

CONTROL OF PESTS AND DISEASES IN LAVENDER

In talking about pests and diseases, this unique plant is justifiably renowned for being remarkably free from pest and disease but they are not entirely immune. There are some few pest to look out for, when growing lavender plants. Whiteflies, aphids, and Spittle bugs can be a nuisance when you grow a lavender plants.

Whiteflies

Lavender is among the numerous plants that attract whiteflies. They feed on the plant sap, although their presence may not necessarily kill your lavender plant, but they can cause unattractive damage to your plant. This are small, powdery insects that are often found on the undersides of the leaves. When their populations are heavy enough, your lavender may show signs of reduced vigour, and her leaves may turned yellowed and mottled. Whiteflies honeydew can also lead to sooty mould.

Controlling Whiteflies

Trying to Control heavy populations of whiteflies could be very difficult at times, this is because they are not effectively controlled with any available insecticides. There are however several natural enemies of whiteflies and these are commercially available. An example is Delphastus pusillus a predatory lady bird beetle which feeds on all stages of whiteflies. Using this controlling method should supplement other biological controls. Another natural means of controlling whiteflies is to hand remove them in order to reduce their populations. Also, spraying lavender with a strong stream of water can help to wash off adult whiteflies from the leaves. When aluminium foil or reflective mulches is applied to the base of the lavender plant, it can be very effective in repelling whiteflies. You can find reflective mulches at most garden centers. Apart from whiteflies, it can also be effective in repelling other pests, such as aphids.

Spittle Bugs

The Spittle Bugs is also referred to as frog hoppers, and they are common pests of lavender plants. They are easily noticeable during the spring, because they secrete a foamy spittle-like substance on your lavender plant. They are unattractive pest, but the bugs rarely reach a level of infestation that will harm the plant's health. In most cases, the stems containing spittle die, and this can lead to an unattractive appearance.

Controlling Spittle Bugs

This pest on lavender plants are usually very easily controlled without the use of pesticides or other chemical treatments. To control spittle bugs in the garden, the best way is to wash your lavender plants periodically with a strong spray of water. Using this method helps to removes both the bugs and the spittle.

Aphids

In themselves, Aphids are not usually directly harmful to your lavender plant, but they however in turn spread alfalfa mosaic virus, which is a common lavender disease. This virus shows as bright yellow patches on leaves and shoots of your plant. In some cases, the infected tissue will become twisted. In as much as this virus affects your plant, it doesn't in most cases kill your lavender plants, alfalfa mosaic virus can reduce the vigour and production of new growth and blooms of your lavender. Plants infected with this virus should be removed and burned to prevent spreading the disease to nearby plants.

How Prevent Alfalfa Mosaic Virus

In preventing this virus in your lavender plant, the best option is to control aphid populations and also to clean and sterilize gardening tools. You can also use horticultural oils and insecticides help reduce aphid populations, while another method is to use natural aphid predators to reduce their populations. Prune out the sections surrounding the plants that has been infested with aphids if possible, and add a reflective mulch or aluminum foil to the base of your lavender plant just to repel aphids.

Cuckoo Spit

This is more of an unattractive nuisance than a real threat to your plant, although the first meal of the green capsid bug growing inside the unpleasant foam will be the lavender plant's sap. The good news is, the solution is simple and does not require chemical. All you need to do is just to spray them away with water.

Shab

This is a fungal disease that affects and kills the branches of lavender plants. The basic symptoms to look out for are shoots that suddenly wilt when there is no drought and stems that turn brown before later developing black spots. Although this is extremely rare in UK and other European gardens, it is also important to be careful and look out for their signs. Plants that are infected should be carefully dug up and burnt.

CHAPTER FIVE

LAVENDER HARVEST

Lavenders are ready for harvest when they have full coloured bud before their individual flowers open. Harvest your lavender when the flowers bloom. Both harvesting and pruning lavender are equally the same. This is when you are removing the flowering stalks from the bush. You have to keep an eye on your lavender in the early spring so that you can catch it right when the flowers open. When this is done, it promotes the growth of new roots in the plant', it also keeps your plant looking neat, and leaves you with about 1 - 8 bunches of fresh lavender flowers. They should be harvested when their flower have just opened within the spring. At this is time, lavender are more beautiful and most fragrant.

When lavender are harvested within the spring, they may have more time to produce more flowers for a second harvest within the year.

In harvesting, you have to gather your lavender plant into a bunch. This is done using your hands to gather as much stalks as possible to fit comfortably in your fist. Lavender stalks are quite hardy, it is therefore possible to gather from all parts of the bush without you worrying about tearing them apart. Within the first-year, your lavender bush will typically produce only enough flowers that can form one to two bunches lavender. A lavender bush can reach its full maturity by the third year of cultivation, at this time, they can produce between 8 to 10 bunches of lavender.

While harvesting, cut your lavender a few inches above the woody growth. Once your lavender has matured, you will notice that it is firmly rooted to the ground with tough, woody growth, and at the top, they grow the green stalks. When you cut your lavender into the woody growth, this can affect your plant. It is therefore important that you cut it about two inches above the end of the woody growth.

While harvesting lavender, the best tool to be used is called a harvesting knife. This knife is curved like a scythe and has a serrated edge. While using this knife, you hook it around the bunched lavender and then pull the knife toward you, cutting off your lavender stalks. Keeping doing this until all the lavender stalks have been cut, and the bush that remains is shaped in a neat-looking mound.

You have to cut your lavender stems in order of blooming. Your first harvest should be early in the flower cycle and as they continue to produce more flowers throughout the season, you cut them when necessary. When you have a smaller variety lavender, they will tend to flower in patches, and should be harvested in timely order that way, so as to encourage re-flowering of your plant. On a general note, lavender will act like any other flowering plant, and when they are de-flowered as early as possible, there will a new flower grows at the base of the flower, giving you more than one harvest in a year.

Take out the dead leaf matter. Cut out all the stalks that are dead, as well as with any stringy twigs and other plant clutter. Doing this, you will almost always be "pruning" for harvest, but in some cases, it is important for you to prune unsightly plant matter at the end of every season. Be careful not to cut into the woody growth.

HOW TO DRY LAVENDER FLOWER

You can dry your lavender on screens or in bunches. In drying your lavender plant, you can make use of a food dehydrator, hang your lavender upside down in to dry in a cool, dark spot at home, or you can dry them outside on screens in the sun. The bunches can then be hung in a place out of the sun and expect them to be dried within 2 weeks. Drying your lavender on screens may affects the colour once they are dried, since time in the sun will lighten it.

Once you choose to hang your lavender plant to dry, use twine or twist ties to gather your lavender stalks together in bunches and hang them upside down on nails or hooks. Retie your stocks when necessary to keep them firmly together, since lavender shrinks while drying. Storing your lavender away from sun and heat will help it to last as long as possible

If you desired, you can de-stem your lavender plant. Smaller variety of lavender usually makes the finest final product, but they also requires additional processing. In order to remove the flowers from the stems, lay your lavender plant between 2 1'x 2' sheets of plywood. Crush and roll the stems in between the wood pieces. Pour your crushed lavender plant through a sieve to catch the flowers.

Lavender can be used in cooking and crafts. Once your lavender is ready and is time to put them to use. Placed your dried stems in vases to decorate your home, use your flowers to make sachets, or use them to make delicious confections with your harvest.

Made in the USA
Coppell, TX
16 July 2020

31137484R00046